CU00660237

HOW TO FIND YOUR PURPOSE

12 Questions That Can CHANGE YOUR ENTIRE LIFE

MICHELLE KULP

Copyright © 2024 by Monarch Crown Publishing
and Michelle Kulp. All Rights Reserved.

No part of this publication may be reproduced, distributed, or
transmitted in any form or by any means, including photocopying,
recording, or other electronic or mechanical methods, or by any
information storage and retrieval system without the prior written
permission of the publisher, except in the case of very brief
quotations embodied in critical reviews and certain other
noncommercial uses permitted by copyright law.

ISBN: 978-1-7373222-8-3

TABLE OF CONTENTS

DEDICATION

To my amazing father who we lost too early (86 years young) who lived his purpose every day of his life! You are an inspiration to me, and your legacy continues. I love you eternally!

INTRODUCTION

One question has the power to completely transform your entire life.

Einstein once said, "If I had an hour to solve a problem and my life depended on the solution, I would spend the first 55 minutes determining the proper question to ask; for once I know the proper question, I could solve the problem in less than five minutes."

Einstein was a brilliant man.

In his #1 Wall Street Journal bestselling book, *The One Thing*, Gary Keller, founder of Keller Williams Realty, Inc., wrote:

"Life is a question. You may be asking, 'Why focus on a question when what we really crave is an answer?' It's simple. Answers come from questions, and the quality of any answer is directly determined by the quality of the question.

Ask the wrong question, get the wrong answer. Ask the right question, get the right answer. Ask the most powerful question possible, and the answer can be life-altering."

Over the years, I, too have learned the power of asking the right questions.

This is a story of a powerful question that changed the trajectory of my life...

On October 23, 1992, I serendipitously met country music singer and actor Billy Ray Cyrus after a concert he performed and I had the pleasure of spending a few hours chatting with him. During our time together, Billy Ray asked me:

"What are your dreams?"

My marriage had recently ended. I was struggling to financially support my three children, living paycheck-to-paycheck working a high-stress job in the legal field,

Severe panic attacks led me to the emergency room, where I thought I was having a heart attack. Additionally, my older brother and best friend, Michael, had been diagnosed with AIDS and was dying. I was only 29 years old at the time.

Needless to say, it was a dark time in my life and I was living in survival mode.

I didn't have the time or energy to think about "dreams."

When you are struggling and in survival mode, you simply don't have the capacity to reflect on higher-level things like *dreams*.

Abraham Maslow spoke about this in his hierarchy of needs, which suggests anyone struggling to get their basic physical or psychological needs met is not in a frame of mind to focus on self-actualization.

MASLOW'S HIERARCHY OF NEEDS

- **Basic (Physiological) Needs** – food, water, warmth, rest

- **Safety Needs** – security, safety

- **Belongingness and Love Needs** – intimate relationships, friends

- **Esteem Needs** – prestige, feeling of accomplishment

- **Self-Actualization** – achieving one's full potential, including creative activities

Billy Ray's question struck a chord deep inside of me. During our conversation, Billy Ray said, "We all have a dream buried inside of us, and it's our job to go out and find that dream and once we do, we must never ever give up on our dream."

I took Billy Ray's advice and went out searching for this elusive dream; the one that would bring me a deep feeling of purpose, passion, and fulfillment; the things that were severely lacking in my life at the time.

It was a year of soul-searching before I figured it out. My breakthrough was triggered by a question I read in a tiny book that fell into my hands at a bookstore, "How to Find Your Mission in Life" by Richard Bolles.

*"What do you love to do
where you lose all sense of time?"*

The moment I read the question, I knew the answer and instantly recognized my dream. I suddenly felt renewed and alive with purpose, passion, and direction in my life.

Pause and think about that question for a few moments before reading on.

When I read that question and reflected on it, my mind drifted back to my childhood, remembering how I loved to write. Five hours seemed like five minutes to me when I was writing poetry, essays, short stories, and even school reports. Writing is where I lost all track of time.

Unfortunately, as we "grow up" and become adults, we leave behind our childhood interests and passions. We tend to choose the more practical path, choosing a job that pays the bills over our soul's aspirations.

The unfortunate part is that when you're stuck in a job you hate, it can feel like you're in a job prison.

I had a job as a paralegal in a high-stress environment for 17 years until I couldn't breathe any longer. It was literally sucking the life out of me.

I wrote about how I freed myself from job prison in my book, *Quit Your Job and Follow Your Dreams: A 12-*

Month Guide to Being Joyfully Jobless. Now, I teach others how to do the same.

Rumi reminds us, "What you are seeking is seeking you."

When Billy Ray Cyrus asked me that question about what my dreams were, it started me down a path that eventually led me to the answer I was looking for.

This book contains 12 life-altering questions. Before we begin, my first question for you is:

Do you listen to your head more than your heart?

Too often, we make decisions solely from our logical minds. That might be okay for a while, but when we are experiencing deep feelings of unhappiness, unfulfillment, and purposelessness, it's time for a change and a new direction.

When we make decisions based purely on logic, we leave our heart and soul out of the equation. When we do that, we often feel depleted, drained as well as mentally, physically, spiritually, and emotionally worn out.

The 12 questions in this book are designed to help you find your Purpose.

Do not rush through the book. Read each chapter, then contemplate your answer to the questions at the end of the chapter and write it out in longhand. Search your heart and soul, and not your logical mind.

Before we dive into the questions, I want to share some tools that I've been using for over 25 years. I believe you can use these tools to help connect your head to your heart while you're on this journey so you can hear the answers deep inside.

TUNING IN TOOLS

I was sitting in my therapist's office when she announced, "I know your problem, Michelle. Your heart and head aren't connected."

She was right. I spent my entire life listening to my "head" while completely ignoring my heart.

My decisions up to that point were practical and based on obligation and responsibility and left my heart out of the equation.

It's been a long arduous journey connecting my heart and my head. Thankfully, I discovered some tools that have helped me along the way. I am sharing those tools with you now so you can use them to receive the same benefits as I have.

Two of the tools (*Morning Pages* and *Artist Date*) I learned about from Julia Cameron, a recovered blocked artist and author of the bestselling book, "The Artist's Way: A Spiritual Path to Higher Creativity."

I'm adding one more tool of my own that will help quiet your egoic mind and help tune you into the whispers of your heart and soul: *meditation.*

It's not required that you use these tools. However, if you are overly practical, responsible, conscientious, and deeply connected to your logical mind like me, I truly believe it will help you tremendously.

Let's begin…

MORNING PAGES

In her book, "The Artist's Way," Julia Cameron introduces two pivotal tools in 'creative recovery' which are the *morning pages* and the *artist's date.*

In order to retrieve your creativity and your passion, you need to find them—morning pages are a vehicle that will help you do that.

Morning pages are three pages of longhand writing, strictly stream-of-consciousness writing. You might think of them as *brain drain*.

There is no wrong way to do the morning pages. They are a primary tool of creative recovery and finding your passion which is part of that creative recovery.

Unfortunately, we are all victims of our inner critic, inner perfectionist, and our inner troublemaker.

This is not the truth of who we are or what we are capable of doing. These collective inner voices are a blocking device that keeps you from your creativity and your passions.

By writing three pages in a notebook or journal every morning, you will get to the other side of your inner censor, troublemaker, and critic.

It doesn't matter what you write about, just write without thinking about what you're writing. No one will see your morning pages so you can vent, complain, cuss, fuss, nag, protest, process, imagine, dream, and invent.

The morning pages will feed your inner artist and you will begin hearing that quiet voice within. Eventually, you will connect with your own quiet center.

The Logical Brain is our survival brain, and it fears the unknown. It tells us to be responsible and sensible always.

The Artist Brain is our creative and holistic brain that wants to come out and play!

Don't underestimate the power of the morning pages as they are a spiritual practice and they will lead you to your inner power and your own source of wisdom.

The only rules are that you write your morning pages as soon as you wake up (stream-of-consciousness writing) and that you write three pages in longhand in a notebook or journal that you do not share with others. That's it.

Morning pages help chart our own inner interior. Without them, our dreams and passions will remain buried.

With consistency, morning pages will point out the need for a *course adjustment.*

Here's what Julia Cameron says about morning pages:

- Your morning pages are your boat. They will both lead you forward and give you a place to recuperate from in your forward motion.

- …writing pages can open an inner door through which our creator helps and guides us. Our willingness swings this inner door open. The morning pages symbolize our willingness to speak to and hear God…it is very powerful.

- The snowflake pattern of your soul is emerging. Each of us is a unique, creative individual. But we often blur that uniqueness with sugar, alcohol, drugs, overwork, underplay bad relations, toxic sex, under-exercise, over-TV, under-sleep—many and varied forms of junk food for the soul. The pages help us to see these smears on our consciousness.

I love what May Sarton, author of dozens of inspirational books including "Journal of a Solitude," says. "It always comes back to the same necessity: go deep enough and there is a bedrock of truth, however hard."

ACTION STEP: Purchase a notebook or journal, label it, and start your morning pages tomorrow.

The next tool up is the artist date...

ARTIST DATE

On the surface, this may seem like a distraction or a diversion, but the artist date is very powerful and is designed to bring you more insight, inspiration, and guidance.

An artist date is a block of time – two hours per week – where you nurture your creative consciousness; your inner artist.

Your artist needs to be taken out, listened to, indulged, and pampered. Think of your inner artist like a child, and the artist date is self-nurturing to your child artist.

When I set aside this time for my artist date, all kinds of emergencies and crises oddly happen that prevent my artist date from happening.

When we are following our passions and purpose, we must fight off a force called "the *resistance*" that does not want us to grow, evolve, or succeed.

Steven Pressfield, the author of several bestselling books like *The War of Art* and *Turning Pro: Tap Your Inner*

Power and Create Your Life's Work explains this resistance we all have to face like this:

"Resistance stops us from committing to the important work of our lives – not just committing to it but fighting like hell to get it done."

He goes on to explain that *the resistance* hates two qualities above all others: Concentration and Depth. *Why?* Because when we work with focus and we work deep, we succeed.

This *resistance* wants us to stay unfocused and shallow. For example, checking social media 50 times a day, getting caught up in other people's drama, watching endless amounts of television, and binging on Netflix instead of doing deep work and activities that are meaningful to our hearts and souls that we are *called* to do.

In her book, "Big Magic," Elizabeth Gilbert, says:

"The universe buries strange jewels deep within us all, and then stands back to see if we can find them.

The hunt to uncover those jewels – that's creative living. The course to go on that hunt in the first place – that's what separates a mundane existence from a more enchanted one."

Just know that when you set aside time for your morning pages and artist dates (your creative work), everything that can block you from using these powerful tools will happen. Don't let it.

Creative living is a path for the brave. It requires courage, persistence, having a daily practice, and moving past your fears.

So, plan your artist date and watch for all kinds of blocks to happen. Rise above them.

Keep your artist date sacred and treat it like an appointment with a Very Important Person, and that VIP is your inner artist child! If you have to reschedule, make sure you put it on the calendar, so you won't forget about it.

Artist Dates don't have to be expensive outings. If you are low on cash, here are some ideas:

- Go to a local park, lake, or beach.

- Go to a pottery place and create art or just observe others.

- Go to a museum.

- Attend an artist event.

- Go to a cooking store and explore.

- Take a hike with beautiful scenery.

- Attend a paint night.

Do any activity that makes your inner artist happy!

ACTION STEP: Schedule your first two artist dates on your calendar and watch the resistance show up and try to block them. Don't let it!

Next up is the final tool – *meditation*.

MEDITATION

Michael Singer, author of the bestselling book "The Untethered Soul," says:

"When you contemplate the nature of Self, you are meditating, that is why meditation is the highest state. It is the return to the root of your being, the simple awareness of being aware."

Meditation halts the incessant chatter in your mind and allows you to connect to your true self. We all possess this "monkey mind" that never stops. When we wake up in the morning, these thoughts take over our minds like little monkeys jumping from tree to tree. Meditation helps the monkey become still and listen.

Meditation is an immensely powerful tool. You can start with a few minutes a day and gradually increase the time. I started with two-minute sessions a day and I now do 20 minutes a day.

Spiritual teacher Pema Chodron, says this about meditation:

"Meditation is a process of lightening up, of trusting the basic goodness of what we have and who we are, and of realizing that any wisdom that exists, exists in what we already have. We can lead our life so as to become more awake to who we are and what we're doing rather than trying to improve or change or get rid of who we are or what we're doing. The key is to wake up, to become more alert, more inquisitive, and curious about ourselves."

~Pema Chodron

Meditation has changed my life, taken away my anxiety, and helped me to connect to my heart and soul.

Meditation is a tool I recommend using as you do this deep work.

ACTION STEP: Download a meditation app and start with 2-5 minutes of meditation today. I use an app called "Chime."

Now it's time to get started on the 12 questions that can change your entire life and help you find your purpose...

CHAPTER 1

MISTAKEN IDENTITY

"False Assumption Number One – 'My job is my mission.' Your job may be and ideally should be part of your mission, but a mission is always larger than a job. Jobs can change—and probably will… To confine the entire sum of your personality and gifts within the boundaries of your current job is to put yourself in the precarious position of losing your sense of identity when your job changes."

~Laurie Beth Jones, "The Path: Creating Your Mission Statement for Work and Life"

In 2000, I was "let go" at the law firm I was working at in Washington DC as a paralegal. I had been feeling unfulfilled for a long time and really wanted out of the legal field which had been draining my spirit and my soul for years, but I didn't know how else to make money to replace that salary.

Losing my job at the law firm was a blessing in disguise because my job had monopolized my time. Once I had my "time" back, I had the freedom to delve into my curiosities, desires, and passions to see what I really wanted to do. I could discover different ways to make a living without giving my soul away.

Through a process of trial and error, I learned what breathed life and energy into me and which ones drained me. I started to follow things that brought me more energy, life, enjoyment, and happiness. It wasn't an overnight journey; I stumbled into clarity over time.

However, I also remember feeling completely lost as my identity as a paralegal was completely stripped from me overnight.

It wasn't only about leaving my title and identity as "paralegal;" it was also about leaving behind the familiarity of my cubicle, daily schedule, commute, co-workers, routines, and all the hours I spent at the office.

I had a blank slate in front of me, and it scared the heck out of me.

Reflect on how your job defines your identity. If tomorrow that job was gone, how would you feel about your life and having this blank slate before you?

I promise you that your job is not your purpose.

QUESTION: How have you made your job your identity? If your job was gone tomorrow, how would that make you feel? What new identity would you like to explore?

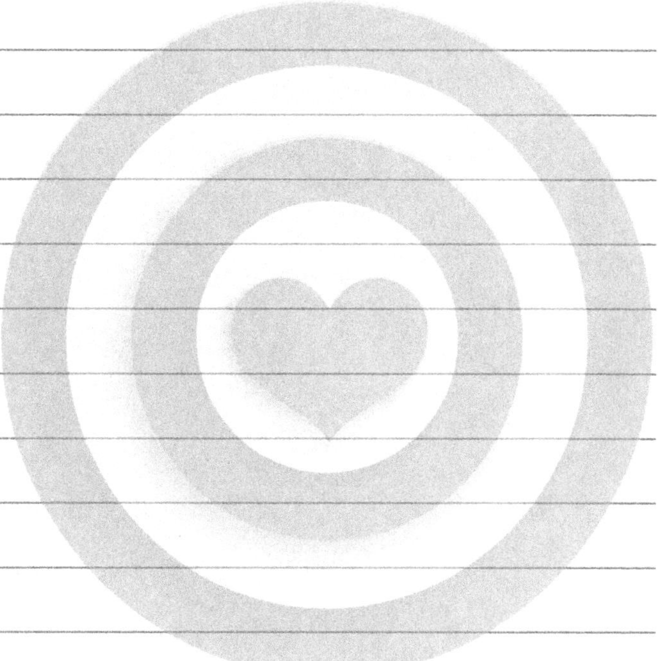

CHAPTER 2

THE CLUE OF STRENGTHS

"Over the past decade, Gallup has surveyed more than 10 million people worldwide on the topic of employee engagement (or how positive and productive people are at work) and only one-third "strongly agree" with the statement: 'At work, I have the opportunity to do what I do best every day." And for those who do not get to focus on what they do best – their strengths – the costs are staggering. In a recent poll of more than 1,000 people, among those who "strongly disagreed" or "disagreed" with this "what I do best" statement, not one single person was emotionally engaged on the job."

~Tom Rath, Author of "Strengths Finder 2.0"

When I was in college getting my degree in pre-law, my two favorite subjects were legal writing and legal research. These subjects stood out among many others that I loved and several that I didn't.

As I look back now, I can see that I was happiest in jobs where I could utilize my strengths (research and writing). Conversely, I was very unhappy and unfulfilled in jobs where I was not using those strengths.

Sometimes we don't even realize what our strengths are.

In my book, "Quit Your Job and Follow Your Dreams," I include an exercise that I call a "Job Autopsy." This involves listing all the tasks you do at work and rating them on a scale from 1-10 (1 being you hate it, and 10 being you love it).

Doing this exercise gives people a lot of insight as to why they "hate" their jobs. It's usually because they are not using their strengths in their job.

I completed the job autopsy after leaving the legal field and discovered that writing and research were not only my strengths, but my gifts.

Within the legal field, I had been a serial job hopper so I could make more money. Unfortunately, this caused me to stray from using my strengths as I was doing a lot of tasks I didn't enjoy. This explains how after nearly two decades in the legal field, I "hated" my job.

As I look back, I didn't hate my job at the beginning of my career because it involved using my strengths, but towards the end of my career, I was not using them at all.

Once I recognized writing as my passion, I pursued that path. Since then, I have written 28 books and counting. I have also found fulfillment in teaching others who want to write, guiding them on how to make a living from their writing.

QUESTION: What are your strengths when it comes to work or your job? If you are unsure, do a job autopsy based on your favorite job, list the tasks involved in that job, and rate each of those tasks to find your strengths.

CHAPTER 3

WHAT MATTERS MOST?

"Things which matter most must never be at the mercy of things which matter least."

~Goethe

When I ask myself what matters most, two things come to mind: Family and Freedom.

I have always been driven by those two things.

However, when I was working 8-12 hour days at the law firm, I didn't have control of my time. Additionally, my income was limited working as a paralegal. On top of that,

I was away from my three children, which as a single mom, wasn't great.

I wanted to be home with my children, but as the sole supporter of my household, I believed I didn't have that luxury since I had to pay the bills.

Thank God I got fired from the law firm and learned about the magic of multiple streams of income, including sales.

I transitioned from legal work to outside sales. Two years after leaving the law firm and discovering that writing was my passion and purpose, I applied for a job as an outside sales rep making 6 figures at a commission-only job working 20 hours a week. Had I known these types of jobs existed, I might have left the legal field much sooner.

Although selling a high-end product as an outside sales representative wasn't my "dream job," it gave me the two things I valued most: Family and Freedom.

I now had the freedom to explore my writing and more time to spend with my kids and that changed everything. With the extra time I never had before, I wrote my first book, launched my first website, and started teaching online classes that brought in multiple streams of income.

QUESTION: What matters most to you? List one or two things. Describe whether your life is designed around what matters most. How can you make what matters most fit into your life?

CHAPTER 4

SAMPLING PERIOD

"Trust the process. A calling calls to remind you to enter the mystery of instinct and the metamorphosis of an inspired life. Honor your passion to emerge."

~Tama Kieves, author of "This Time I Dance: Trusting the Journey of Creating the Work Your Love"

When my identity was stripped away from me after 17 long years in the legal field, I felt I desperately needed a new identity. Like instantly. Like tomorrow. I felt naked without my old identity.

Unfortunately, creating an inspired life and a life of purpose takes time.

Why?

Two words: "Sampling Period."

In his book, "Range: Why Generalists Triumph in a Specialized World," author David Epstein, talking about successful athletes, says:

"Eventual elites typically devote less time early on to deliberate practice in the activity in which they will eventually become experts. Instead, they undergo what researchers call a "sampling period." They play a variety of sports, usually in an unstructured or lightly structured environment; they gain a range of physical proficiencies from which they can draw; they learn about their own abilities and proclivities; and only later do they focus in and ramp up technical practice in one area."

To sum it up, Epstein says it is very common to have a sampling period and he calls this: late specialization.

We need "time" to explore; we need time to observe and try out new things. Life is a journey, not a destination, and so is finding your purpose and passions and creating an inspired life.

During my "sampling period" after leaving my job, I tried dozens of new things such as:

- Working on my public speaking skills (I hated public speaking). Eventually, however, I became area governor of the National Speakers Association and a certified facilitator of Speaking Circles®.

- Working in sales positions for different types of companies such as: Hot Tubs and Swim Spas, HVAC, Windows, Bath Fitter, Gutter Guards, Remodeling, and more.

- Becoming a freelance Newspaper Reporter for *The Capital Gazette Newspaper.*

- Starting a website and offering different services such as website design, copywriting services, ghostwriting, coaching and selling online programs. I also offered done for your packages on my website: www.bestsellingauthorprogram.com

I didn't realize it at the time because I wanted to figure it all out right away, but these few years were my sampling period.

Eventually, I hired my first high-ticket business coach in 2014. He looked at my website and said "Michelle, I don't know what you do. You have several different offers. If you want to work with me you need to pick one thing."

Picking one thing seemed like the hardest thing in the world for me. However, my coach wouldn't work with me if I wouldn't focus on one offer. Finally, I chose something I loved the most – writing.

At the time, I had a 6-week online course called "How to Become a Bestselling Author" that I was selling for $197. After taking the course, most people needed more help achieving the results they wanted. My coach helped me turn that low ticket online course into a high ticket done-for-you service starting at $5K. Since then, the price has increased substantially.

I am grateful for my sampling period and I wish I would have allowed myself the time to be in the unknown.

QUESTION: What does an Inspired Life look like to you? List all the details. Have you ever given yourself a sampling period to explore different things to see what brings you joy and energy? If not, how can you allow yourself more time to explore?

CHAPTER 5

SUCCESS TRAPS

"When I first left law, I stayed in my same apartment, but later I knew I wanted to shrink my expenses instead of my opportunities. For weeks I scanned the paper's ads for places to live. I needed a cheap place to prolong my freedom from full-time, high responsibility work. I kept reminding myself… 'The fewer dollars I have to pay, the more time I have to play."

~Tama Kieves, author of "This Time I Dance"

Many people think cutting down on material items equates to deprivation, limitation, or scarcity.

Think about what Tama said, "The fewer dollars I have to pay, the more time I have to play."

When I left my $50K salary in 2000, I had to reduce my expenses so I could have more freedom. Also, I did not want to have to find another soul-sucking job to pay the bills.

I refinanced my house to lower my mortgage payment and removed expenses that were "wants" and not "needs." It was hard at first, but it took the pressure off believing the only answer was to get another 9-5 job.

You might be thinking the same thing that I thought at the time, "I can't leave my job because I have to pay the bills." But if you hate your job, you do have other options.

Reducing your expenses will give you that extra cushion so you can explore your curiosities and see where those lead.

I didn't love, or even like, everything I tried. I actually hated public speaking, but this little voice inside my head kept saying, "Michelle, if you don't get over your fear of public speaking, you will never become a successful writer."

I was unsure what public speaking had to do with being a writer at the time, but now I see why I needed those skills. Because I love teaching and that involves public speaking.

I've heard making a lot of money referred to as "Golden Handcuffs," and I get it.

Often those who earn a higher salary tend to create a lifestyle that matches that higher salary, essentially "golden handcuffs" that can be hard to escape from.

I'm sure that's why "Tiny Homes," being a "Digital Nomad," and "Living the RV Life" have taken off.

To break free from golden handcuffs, many people had to eliminate their huge expenses and downsize in a BIG way.

**QUESTION: If you could reduce your expenses by 25%
or 50%, what would that mean to your life and being
able to make other choices that honor your desires?
How could you do that?**

CHAPTER 6

YOUR INNER & OUTER PURPOSE

"As soon as you rise above mere survival, the question of meaning and purpose becomes of paramount import- ance in your life. Many people feel caught up in the routines of daily living that seem to deprive their life of significance... Some are consumed by acute stress, others by acute boredom. Some are lost in frantic doing; others are lost in stagnation. Many people long for the freedom and expansion that prosperity promises... There is no substitute for finding true purpose... Your inner purpose is to awaken. It is as simple as that. Your outer purpose can change over time.

Finding and living in alignment with the inner purpose is the foundation for fulfilling your outer purpose. It is the basis for true success."

~Eckhart Tolle, Author of
"A New Earth: Awakening to Your Life's Purpose"

There is a lot of terminology when it comes to feeling lost and unfulfilled – finding your mission, finding your calling, finding your passion, finding your purpose.

Over the years, I've done a lot of work in these areas and I've taught others in some of these areas.

I love the simplicity of Eckhart Tolle's teaching about inner and outer purpose:

- Inner Purpose = To Awaken

- Outer Purpose = Finding and living in alignment with your inner purpose knowing that this will change over time.

Knowing that I am living my purpose of "awakening" every day is very satisfying to me.

I don't need to frantically try to find some elusive purpose. As long as I am not living in survival mode, I have the time to use the tools of self-discovery that I mentioned in the Introduction (morning pages, artist dates, and meditation). These tools will lead me to waking up to my curiosities, desires and dreams about my life.

This is not a one-and-done event. We change over time and so these things also change over time.

Your purpose is simply to awaken and connect to that inner voice that will guide you so you can live an authentic life.

Your outer purpose, which will change over time, is living in alignment with what you "awaken" to.

For example, if I am awakening and realize I can no longer be happy working in my 9-5 job, then my outer purpose is to discover a way out of that job and create something new that is more in alignment with who I am so I can live authentically.

When I finally got out of living in survival mode working at the law firm, I had the gift of time that allowed me try on so many different hats.

Finding your Purpose is more about trying out new things while you are "awakening" and seeing what brings you excitement and energy.

Writing is my obsession. I love it so much that I'm writing a book a month again this year, just like I did in 2020. It brings me purpose, profits and joy.

When you explore new things, you will figure out what you love and what your obsession is.

But you'll never find it if you keep doing the same thing over and over.

It takes courage to break free from the box we've put ourselves in, but you hold the keys to your prison. It's time to break out.

QUESTION: Are you living in survival mode? If so, your first goal is to stop living in survival mode so you can move to the second goal — exploring and trying new things. List 10 NEW things you would love to explore (hobbies, interests, skills, jobs, business, etc.).

CHAPTER 7

MEET YOUR RESISTANCE

"I know one simple, surefire way to make your resistance come out into the open: Start moving toward a goal you really want, and the resistance will leap out of hiding and start trying to talk you out of moving… Your resistance will stay dormant as long as you're not threatening it. But it will wake up fast the second you start moving and announce itself loudly: 'What are you doing!?' 'You're going to get in trouble.' 'This isn't for you.' 'This is a stupid idea.' 'You're going to fail'… Take a closer look. This little troublemaker thinks it is defending you by doing everything in its power to discourage you every time it senses danger—and it senses danger every time you reach for what you want."

**~Barbara Sher, author of
"I Could Do Anything If I Only Knew What It Was"**

Resistance is real, tenacious, and steadfast.

Whenever you start to try something new, resistance rears its ugly head.

In 2020 when I set the audacious goal of writing a book a month for a year as an experiment, all hell broke loose.

My daughter broke up with her ex and she and my two-year-old granddaughter moved back home with me. Instead of having a quiet place to do my writing, I had an active two-year-old in my home.

So, I tried to quit. That's actually what resistance wants you to do. To give up.

It says things like:

"It's not the right time."

"I'll get back to this later when things settle down."

"This is never going to work. I don't know why I even tried."

Luckily for me, I opened my big mouth and told not only my family and friends that I was writing a book a month, but I also told my clients and my email list of 5000 people.

I couldn't quit because everyone was asking me how my experiment was going. This public accountability saved me from quitting. Otherwise, I definitely would have quit because I felt like I had a valid reason.

I'm happy to say I pushed through the resistance.

It was extremely difficult the first few months, and I wanted to quit 100 times, but I kept at it. I found that having this deadline of 30 days was the best thing ever.

Before 2020, I wrote books sporadically every few years. Most of my time was spent helping my clients write, publish, and launch their books to the bestsellers list. To date, I've helped over 500 people become published authors.

With this 30-day deadline and public accountability, I was finally able to get my books written and published. I developed a system for it. In fact, I teach my BAM (book a month) system in my 8-week online program, called "Digital Retirement Academy."

I've had over 100 people go through the program and I warn them all about resistance.

Many of them are dealing with the resistance as soon as they sign up for my program. Remember, resistance doesn't want anything to change and it doesn't want you to try new things.

It loves the status quo.

Resistance can come in many forms, not just your inner negative voice/troublemaker giving you 100 excuses why you shouldn't do this new thing. It brings new situations and obstacles into your life to deter you from moving forward.

In 2023, I start writing a book a month, publishing books in January, February, and March. Then my 86-year-old dad who is my best friend and the light of my life, got very sick very quickly. I put everything on hold to care for him until he passed away in May. Obviously, it is okay, to put things on hold to care for a family member, but I never started writing again in 2023. I was dealing with a lot of grief and heartache.

Now it's 2024 and I'm back at it. The key is to never give up and to remember, resistance doesn't want you to just "pause" or "take a break." Its goal is to get you to quit all together.

So, even though we sometimes have to pause when unexpected events and circumstances show up in our lives, we must resume when the time is right.

And who knows, maybe if I had continued writing that would have helped me through a difficult time.

QUESTION: Was there a time in your life when you found the courage to reach for something new and resistance reared its ugly head? Write about how resistance showed up in your life during a significant time or event. Then, I want you rewrite your past. Look over this event and imagine everything happened differently. Perhaps you had stayed on course, taken your big shot, and hit it. Where would you be now?

_____

_____

_____

_____

_____

_____

_____

_____

_____

_____

_____

_____

CHAPTER 8

MUCH TO-DO
ABOUT NOTHING

"As Henry David Thoreau said, 'It's not enough to be busy, so are the ants. The question is, what are we busy about?' Knocking out a hundred tasks for whatever reason is a poor substitute for doing even one task that's meaningful. Not everything matters equally, and success isn't a game won by whoever does the most. Yet that is exactly how most play it on a daily basis... While to do lists serve as a useful collection of our best intentions, they also tyrannize us with trivial, unimportant stuff that we feel obligated to get done—because it's on our list... Most inboxes overflow with unimportant emails masquerading as priorities. But, as Australian prime

minister Bob Hawke duly notes, 'The things which are most important don't always scream the loudest.'"

~Gary Keller, author of
"The One Thing: The Surprisingly Simple
Truth Behind Extraordinary Results"

Gary Keller writes extensively about to-do lists in his book, "The One Thing" and goes on to say, "To-do lists tend to be long; success lists are short."

For a while, I would write "To-Done" lists, including everything I completed that day to make myself feel productive. Here's an example:

√   Washed, dried, and folded laundry

√   Went to the grocery store

√   Called Insurance company

√   Looked for an MVA title for my daughter

√   Called the bank about an unauthorized charge

√   Washed dishes

√   Cleaned out fridge

√   Called a friend

√   Blah, blah, blah

The point is this long list tended to be more about chores and adding every little thing I did on it so I could feel productive at the end of the day.

If you compare that to a "success list", what would that have looked like?

Right now, I have one goal for the month—to complete this book so I can send it over to editing, formatting, and getting my cover designed. Then, I will move on to the next month's book as I am writing a book a month this year.

So, my success list would have one thing on it:

• Write for three hours on January book

I've decided that writing for three hours a day works best for me. I didn't start out with three hours, but I gradually increased my focus time from one hour to two hours to three hours.

Yesterday I wrote the first six chapters of this book in three hours because I had zero distractions and because I write for three hours straight and can focus on one thing.

What works for me right now is I have two to do lists and it is divided into business and personal. At the top of each of those to-do lists are three most important things I must do today and those are built on my success list.

My success list currently is writing a book a month and soon I will add creating an automated webinar for my program Digital Retirement Academy.

QUESTION: Look at your current to-do list. If you're to-do list contains everything, then it's probably taking you everywhere but where you really want to go. Rewrite your to-do list. Break it down into two sections: business/work and personal. Write one success item on each side (this could be a goal, an interest, or a dream you have). Every day you will work on that success list before working on your to-do list.

CHAPTER 9

ELIMINATE, THEN DELEGATE

"Getting a remote personal assistant is a huge departure point and marks the moment that you learn how to give orders and be commander instead of the commanded… Becoming a member of the New Rich is not just about working smarter. It's about building a system to replace yourself… Because the goal is to free your time to focus on bigger and better things. Few do it, which is another reason so few people have their ideal lifestyles… Did I mention eliminate before you delegate?

~Timothy Ferris, author of "The 4-Hour Workweek: Escape 9-5, Live Anywhere and Join the New Rich

The two biggest reasons people have for not achieving their dreams and goals are time and money.

This chapter is about your time and where it is going.

Until you know what you are spending your time on, it's easy to say you don't have enough time. But that's not true.

You would have enough time if you could eliminate tasks that were wasting your time and delegate those to others so you had more time to focus on your goals and dreams.

When I was trying to build my online business, I was spending a lot of time cleaning my house. With three teenagers, which was an endless task.

At first, I didn't think I could afford a cleaning company. Then I realized how much my time was worth and how much of my valuable time I was spending cleaning.

If my time was worth $250 per hour and I was doing $25 per hour tasks, that was not a good use of my time.

So, I took the plunge and hired a cleaning company, freeing up a lot of my time.

Next, I hired a personal assistant to help me with business and personal tasks.

His name was Felix, and I met him at the mall. He was working at a little shop and we became friends. One day, he got fired from his job and I decided to hire him, paying him $12 per hour. (This was many years ago), but I can't tell you how that changed my life!

Felix loved to shop, decorate, run errands, travel, and was good with social media. I employed him for about a year and it made my life so much easier.

Unfortunately, he moved back to his home town and I lost my personal assistant. I still miss him to this day.

Now I have a Virtual Assistant who focuses 100% on business tasks for me and she is amazing. She is $25 per hour and worth it.

QUESTION: Think about things you can eliminate and delegate. List five items you can eliminate from your life that will give you back your time. Now list five things you can delegate that will also give you back more of your time. What will you spend that extra time on?

CHAPTER 10

DELIBERATE PRACTICE

"When experts exhibit their superior performance in public their behavior looks so effortless and natural that we are attempted to attribute it to special talents... However when scientists began measuring the experts' supposedly superior powers...no general superiority was found... It is a lifetime accumulation of deliberate practice that again and again ends up explaining excellence... Deliberate practice might provide the key to quickly becoming so good they can't ignore you."

Cal Newport, author of
"So Good They Can't Ignore You"

I stumbled into the concept of deliberate practice by accident.

I was unaware it was a "thing" when I decided to write a book a month in 2020 as an experiment.

I realized that all my time was spent working with clients to help them get their books written, published and launched while neglecting my own dreams of writing books.

Coincidentally, around the same time, I came across a blog post on Written Word Media. It said that said the average author who earns six figures in royalties typically has 28 books in their catalogue.

This inspired me to test this theory and write a book a month to see how much passive income I could create with my books.

Surprisingly, by the end of this 12-month experiment, I was making $3335 per month, exceeding my social security income.

Then, I wrote a book about my experiment. Several people who wanted to do the same thing reached out to me and that's how *Digital Retirement Academy* was born!

Deliberate practice is the key to becoming *so good they can't ignore you*.

Now, because I put in the time and practice to write a book a month, I have developed a multiple 6-figure online business.

And you know what happened after 12 months of writing a book a month?

- My writing improved

- I developed a system for writing a book a month

- I wrote books that changed lives

- I grew my following and audience

- I created multiple streams of income from this one practice of writing a book a month

- My discipline grew

- My priorities changed

- I learned to eliminate tasks and delegate more

- I laid the foundation for a 7-figure business

People are rarely overnight successes. They have usually put in at least 10,000 hours, if not more, into their practice.

Take Jerry Seinfeld for example. He didn't accidentally become an overnight success. He learned the art of deliberate practice. Every day, he would write one joke based on an observation. Then, he would draw an "x" on the calendar. He didn't want to break the chain of "x's", so he continued with this deliberate practice, which led to his massive success.

QUESTION: If you want to become "so good they can't ignore you," in what area of your life can you create a new deliberate practice? If you do anything for one year, it will transform your life. Write down the deliberate practice you want to focus on in the next year.

CHAPTER 11

CHILL

"The universe is always tugging us in the direction of our dharma (purpose), through excitement and curiosity. We must remain open to the pull. Most of us are busy pushing that when the universe tells us "Google that; take that workshop; learn from that person." Your job is to listen. Honor your curiosities as if they were gems given to you by the universe. They carry information you need to get to the next step. And sometimes that next step isn't a full-blown career. Sometimes you just needed to learn something, experience something, try something. Sometimes your dharma requires us to do something just for the love of it for years to gain the experience before we're ready to share it…

Not all your interests have to turn into your career. Discovering your dharma is not about monetizing every one of your hobbies. In today's entrepreneurial-focused environment, we often start daydreaming about what a career as a backup dancer might look like because we went to one class. Chill. You can still do things for fun without them going on your resume."

~Sahara Rose, author of "Discover Your Dharma: A Vedic Guide to Finding Your Purpose"

I wish I had known this a long time ago. I was always trying to turn my interests into a business. I have always had a very entrepreneurial mindset since I was a child making money babysitting at age 13, locating lost animals for a finder's fee, and putting on neighborhood skits.

As I got older, once I left the legal field and had to figure out ways to replace that income, I tried out a lot of different things to make money:

- I ran a roommate matching service (before the Internet existed)

- I sold candles

- I sold Christmas products

- I was involved in an MLM

- I did private process serving

- I had a legal word-processing company

- And the list goes on

At one point, I started reading books about feng shui, which was fascinating to me, so I considered signing up to become a certified feng shui practitioner. Feng shui is the Chinese art of the placement of furniture and decor in your home or business. I'm glad I didn't because that would have led me down a whole other path.

We need to learn to have fun and listen to what our intuition is telling us. Sometimes we are being nudged to do things just to learn to relax or to connect with certain people.

You can have fun without starting a business or trying to make money at it.

Having a creative space to play helps us figure out our next steps. We don't need to see the whole staircase to take the next step. It's about trusting our intuition.

Think about children who love to play and are very creative. Like children, we need to allow ourselves to have fun and play without a serious destination in mind.

I love what Elizabeth Gilbert, author of "Big Magic: Creative Living Beyond Fear," says in her book:

"My father decided that he didn't merely want to be a chemical engineer; he also wanted to be a Christmas tree farmer, and so in 1973 he went and did that. He moved us out to a farm, cleared some land, planted some seedlings and commenced with his project. He didn't quit his day job to follow his dream; he just folded his dream into his everyday life. He wanted to raise goats, too, so he acquired some goats. Brought them home in the back seat of our Ford Pinto. Had he ever raised goats? No, but he thought he could figure it out. It was the same thing when he became interested in beekeeping. He just got himself some bees and began. Thirty-five years later, he still has those hives."

QUESTION: What are you interested in right now? What would you love to practice but feel you don't have time for? How can you fold this interest into your everyday life just for fun?

CHAPTER 12

DO NOT KILL THE VOID

"The pure space has a magnetism that reaches deep inside our being and brings out the best part of us, the part ready to be born. There was nothing... then there is something. The void must be treated with respect, entered carefully and slowly. If the void is filled thoughtlessly, it's power is destroyed and a precious potential is lost. Covering new space too quickly, either for reassurance or for practicality, will smother your intuition. Let yourself rest in the void for a while. Live with the uncertainty of what will appear in the surrounding white space... Hidden levels reveal themselves when you rest quietly in the unknown.

**~Michele Cassou and Stewart Cuble, authors of
"Life, Paint and Passion: Reclaiming the
Magic of Spontaneous Express"**

I was very uncomfortable with the void after being fired from my job at the law firm. After 17 years, I didn't know who I was, but I knew one thing… I needed to find a new identity fast.

The first year, I had a tremendous amount of anxiety because I didn't know how to navigate the void of my life. I even ended up in the emergency room one day thinking I was having a heart attack. After several tests, including an EKG, doctors determined I had a lot of stress in my life and my chest pain was caused by anxiety. So, they referred me to a psychiatrist.

Now that I am 60 years old and a bit wiser, I know that we have different seasons in our lives.

In one of my favorite books, "Wintering: The Power of Rest and Retreat in Difficult Times," author Katherine May says:

"Everybody winters at one time or another; some winter over and over again.

Wintering is a season in the cold. It is a fallow period in life when you're cut off from the world, feeling rejected, side-lined, blocked from progress, or cast into the role of an outsider. Perhaps it results from an illness or a life event such as bereavement or the birth of a child; perhaps it comes from a humiliation or failure. Perhaps you're in a period of transition and have temporarily fallen between two worlds. Some winterings creep upon us more slowly, accompanying the protracted death of a relationship, the gradual ratcheting up of caring responsibilities as our parents age, the drip-drip-drip of lost confidence. Some are appallingly sudden, like discovering one day that your skills are considered obsolete, the company you worked for has gone bankrupt, or your partner is in love with someone new. However it arrives, wintering is usually involuntarily, lonely and deeply painful… Yet it's also inevitable."

As I read Katherine's book for the second time, I realize I have been in this wintering season many times.

- When my ex-fiancée' of eight years cheated on me and we broke up

- When my marriage ended

- When my legal career ended

- When my kids moved out

- When I moved into a home that I felt deep down I wasn't deserving of

- When my father, my best friend, passed away

Again, I wish back then I had known about these periods of "wintering" that come to visit all of us.

Interestingly, animals don't fight the winter. Instead, they prepare for it. They perform many extraordinary acts of metamorphosis to survive the winter.

Winter is a time when we withdraw from the world, but it's also a time of transformation.

Once we stop wishing it was summer or spring and we accept this time of wintering, we can reflect, nourish ourselves and put ourselves back together.

This takes time. It doesn't happen overnight. When we try to force ourselves out of winter, it usually doesn't work.

Wintering is about facing the void. What may have worked before, or what was before, has changed. Things are different now.

Looking at my list above of the events that caused me to go into this void, this wintering season, you'll notice they were big changes in my life and usually endings.

As you are beginning to get in touch with your inner voice—your intuition, your internal guide—expect endings. Right now, you probably have things that you must end in order to transition into the next season of your life.

Be prepared for winter and don't try to resist it. It's coming to you because a metamorphosis is on the horizon.

Embrace the Void.

QUESTION: What needs to end in your life right now so you can move to that next stage, whether in your personal relationships, business, job, health, living space, or spirituality?

Explain why you have been putting off ending this part of your life and how you can move into that ending so you can grow and evolve. This is why we are here. To grow. To change. To awaken.

_____

_____

_____

_____

_____

_____

_____

_____

_____

_____

_____

ABOUT MICHELLE KULP

Michelle Kulp left a 17-year career in the legal field to follow her dreams of writing, teaching and speaking. She started her first website in 2005, to inspire women to live their passions, follow their dreams, and make 6 figures doing what they love!

Since 2013, Michelle has been helping authors write, publish, and launch books to the Amazon, Wall Street Journal, and USA Today bestsellers list. To date, she's helped over 500 authors get their books published and become #1 bestselling authors.

Additionally, Michelle has written, published, and launched a book a month for an entire year in 2020 and now has over 28 bestselling books. Michelle now teaches others how to write a book a month and create their own digital Retirement through her #1 bestselling book *Digital Retirement* and her signature program "Digital Retirement Academy". Michelle offers a variety of programs and courses for CEOs, Entrepreneurs, and Business Owners to help them strategize, and then write and launch their books to the world!

You can connect with Michelle at:
www.bestsellingauthorprogram.com

OTHER BOOKS BY MICHELLE KULP

Some of Michelle's bestselling books are:

How to Find Your Passion:
https://www.amazon.com/How-Find-Your-Passion-Questions-ebook/dp/B083XL67GZ

Digital Retirement:
https://www.amazon.com/Digital-Retirement-Replace-Social-Security-ebook/dp/B08KBXZMJN

Six Figure Author Series:
https://www.amazon.com/Six-Figure-Author-Backwards-Launch-ebook/dp/B0973FB3CD

You can see all of Michelle's books here:

https://www.amazon.com/stores/Michelle-Kulp/author/B006D4EQIY

Please consider leaving a review as it helps me tremendously and can really improve the sales of the books and the author's life!

Printed in Great Britain
by Amazon

44439020R00056